Whispers Of Shadows

BY COREY BENNETT

CONTENTS

Chapter 1: The Enchanted Night

The village of Eldenwood, nestled deep within an ancient forest, was a place where magic and mystery intertwined. Elara, a young woman with striking emerald eyes and a cascade of raven-black hair, had always felt like an outsider. She had grown up listening to tales of the forest's enchantments, yet the whispers she heard in her dreams seemed far more real.

Elara's nights were haunted by visions of a shadowy figure, a man whose eyes glowed with an othe

rworldly light. She would wake up with her heart racing, the whisper of his voice lingering in her mind. She couldn't shake the feeling that these dreams were calling her to something—or someone—important.

One fateful night, drawn by an inexplicable urge, Elara ventured into the forest. The moon hung low, casting an eerie glow through the dense canopy. The forest seemed alive, with every rustle and creak heightening her senses. As she walked deeper, the air grew colder, and she felt an invisible force guiding her steps.

Suddenly, she saw him—the figure from her dreams. He stood in a small clearing, his presence commanding and ethereal. His hair was as dark as the night, and his eyes, a striking violet, seemed to pierce through her soul.

"Who are you?" Elara whispered, her voice trembling.

"I am Malachi," he replied, his voice a deep, resonant timbre. "And you, Elara, are the one I've been searching for."

Confusion and curiosity warred within her. "How do you know my name?"

Malachi stepped closer, his gaze never leaving hers. "Because our fates are intertwined. I am a prince, cursed to roam the night, bound by dark magic. You are the key to breaking that curse."

Elara felt a shiver run down her spine. She should have been afraid, but something about Malachi drew her in. His curse, his pain—it resonated with the emptiness she had always felt.

"I don't understand," she said, shaking her head.

"All will be revealed in time," Malachi assured her. "But know this: your dreams were no mere coincidence. They were a call—a call to destiny."

As the night wore on, Malachi explained his plight. Long ago, he had been betrayed by those he trusted, leading to his imprisonment in a shadowy realm. Only the power of true love, combined with ancient magic, could set him free. Elara's heart ached for him, and she found herself drawn to his strength and vulnerability.

When dawn approached, Malachi's form began to waver. "I must go," he said, his voice tinged with regret. "But I will return, Elara. Until then, remember: you are not alone."

Elara watched as he disappeared into the mist, her mind reeling with the revelations of the night. As she made her way back to the village, she knew her life had changed forever. The enchanted night had awakened something within her—something powerful and undeniable.

Chapter 2: Secrets Unveiled

The days following her encounter with Malachi were a blur of anticipation and anxiety. Elara found it hard to focus on her daily tasks, her mind constantly drifting to the mysterious prince and his haunting eyes. She couldn't shake the feeling that her dreams held more significance than she had ever imagined.

One evening, as the sun dipped below the horizon, Elara felt a familiar tug at her heart. She made her way back to the clearing where she had first met Malachi, hoping to find answers to the questions that plagued her.

As if summoned by her thoughts, Malachi appeared, his presence as mesmerising as ever. He greeted her with a gentle smile, his eyes reflecting the moonlight. "I'm glad you came."

Elara nodded, her curiosity burning. "I need to understand. How are our fates connected? What does it mean that I'm the key to breaking your curse?"

Malachi took a deep breath, his expression serious. "Many years ago, my family ruled this land. But jealousy and greed led to our downfall. A powerful sorceress, Lilith, coveted our kingdom and cast a dark spell upon me. I was cursed to wander the night, trapped between worlds, until true love could break the enchantment."

He paused, his gaze softening as he looked at Elara. "Your dreams, Elara, are a manifestation of our connection. Your lineage is tied to ancient magic, and within you lies the power to break my curse."

Elara's mind raced as she tried to process his words. "But why me? I'm just an ordinary girl from Eldenwood."

Malachi shook his head. "You are far from ordinary. Your ancestors were powerful sorcerers, and their blood runs through your veins. You possess untapped potential, a magic that resonates with mine."

As they spoke, Elara began to sense a strange energy coursing through her. It was as if a dormant power within her was awakening, responding to Malachi's presence. She realized that her dreams had not been mere fantasies—they were glimpses of a destiny she had yet to fully comprehend.

Determined to understand her newfound abilities, Elara sought out the village's oldest and wisest inhabitant, an elder named Gertrude. Known for her knowledge of the arcane, Gertrude had always been a source of guidance and wisdom.

When Elara confided in her, Gertrude's eyes widened with recognition. "I had suspected there was something special about you, child. Your family's history is steeped in magic, though much of it has been forgotten over the generations."

Elara listened intently as Gertrude recounted tales of her ancestors, sorcerers who had once protected Eldenwood from dark forces. She spoke of ancient prophecies and the power of true love to break even the most formidable curses.

"You must embrace your heritage, Elara," Gertrude advised. "The magic within you is strong, and it will only grow stronger with time and practice. Malachi's fate is indeed tied to yours.

Chapter 3: Forbidden Love

As Elara and Malachi's journey continued, their bond grew deeper, transforming into a love that defied the very nature of their worlds.

Each night spent together brought new revelations and an undeniable connection that neither could ignore. But with their love came an ever-growing danger, as the forces that sought to keep them apart grew more determined.

In the village of Eldenwood, whispers of their forbidden romance spread, fueled by the elder's lingering distrust. The villagers, though supportive of Elara's quest, couldn't shake their unease about her relationship with the cursed prince. They saw their love as a harbinger of more dark magic and trouble.

One evening, as the moon cast its silver glow over the forest, Elara and Malachi found solace in a hidden grove, far from prying eyes. They sat together beneath an ancient oak, the air filled with the soft hum of night creatures.

Malachi turned to Elara, his eyes reflecting the moonlight. "Our love is a dangerous thing, Elara. It defies the natural order and the curse that binds me."

Elara reached out, her fingers brushing his cheek. "I don't care about the danger, Malachi. What we have is real, and I won't let anything come between us."

He took her hand in his, his grip firm but gentle. "We must be careful. Lilith's spies are everywhere, and the villagers' fear makes them unpredictable. We need to find the Heart of Shadows soon, before our enemies can strike.

Determined to protect their love and break the curse, they continued their search with renewed urgency. Their journey led them to forgotten ruins and ancient temples, where they faced trials that tested their resolve and their bond.

One night, as they explored an abandoned temple deep in the heart of the forest, they encountered a creature of darkness, a guardian of the secrets they sought.

The battle was fierce, but with Elara's growing magical prowess and Malachi's strength, they emerged victorious.

As the creature lay defeated, Elara noticed an inscription on the temple wall, written in a language she barely understood. She traced the runes with her fingers, feeling the magic thrumming beneath the surface.

"These runes… they speak of the Heart of Shadows," she murmured. "It's hidden within the deepest part of the forest, guarded by ancient magic."

Malachi stepped closer, his eyes scanning the inscription. "We're getting closer, Elara. But the closer we get, the more dangerous it becomes. We must be prepared for anything."

Their journey continued, filled with peril and moments of profound connection. Each obstacle they overcame brought them closer to their goal and to each other. Their love, once forbidden and fraught with danger, became a beacon of hope and strength.

But as they neared their destination, the elder's suspicions turned to outright hostility. He rallied the villagers, convincing them that Elara's love for Malachi was a threat to their safety. Fearful and manipulated, the villagers agreed to confront Elara once more.

On the eve of their final journey into the deepest part of the forest, Elara and Malachi returned to the village, seeking rest and supplies. They were met with hostility and suspicion, the elder's words having sown deep mistrust.

"You cannot go on," the elder declared, blocking their path. "Your love has brought nothing but darkness upon us."

Elara stood tall, her voice unwavering. "Our love is what will break the curse and save us all. Do not let fear blind you to the truth."

But the elder would not be swayed. "If you continue on this path, you will be exiled. We cannot risk the safety of the village for your foolish quest."

With heavy hearts, Elara and Malachi left Eldenwood, knowing they could not return until the curse was broken. Their love, though forbidden and fraught with danger, was their guiding light as they ventured into the darkest part of the forest.

Together, they faced the shadows, determined to break the curse and forge a future where their love could flourish in the light.

Chapter 4: Shadows of the Past

The dense canopy of the forest grew thicker as Elara and Malachi ventured deeper into the heart of darkness. The air was heavy with an ancient, oppressive magic that seemed to pulse with malevolent intent. Despite the danger, Elara felt a strange sense of familiarity, as if the forest itself held the echoes of her ancestors.

As they pressed on, they stumbled upon an old, crumbling cottage hidden beneath the twisted branches. Elara felt an inexplicable pull towards it, a whisper of something long forgotten. Inside, they found relics of a time when magic was openly practiced—old spell books, potions, and talismans.

Malachi picked up a weathered journal, its pages brittle with age. "This must have belonged to your ancestors," he said, handing it to Elara.

She opened the journal carefully, her eyes scanning the faded ink. The entries were filled with notes on powerful spells, ancient rituals, and, to her surprise, mentions of a prophecy. Her heart raced as she read the words:

"One will come, born of our blood, who holds the power to break the curse of shadows. Through love and sacrifice, the darkness shall be vanquished, and the realm restored."

Elara looked up at Malachi, her eyes wide with realization. "This prophecy… it's about us. My ancestors knew that one day, someone from our line would have the power to break your curse."

Malachi nodded, his expression a mix of hope and determination. "Then we are on the right path. We must find the Heart of Shadows and fulfill this prophecy."

With renewed purpose, they continued their journey, guided by the knowledge of the past. Each step brought them closer to the source of Lilith's power and the promise of breaking Malachi's curse.

As they ventured deeper, the forest grew darker, the air thick with an ominous presence. Shadows seemed to move on their own, whispering secrets that only Elara could hear. Her dreams became more vivid, filled with images of Lilith and the Heart of Shadows. She felt a strange connection to the dark sorceress, as if their fates were inexplicably linked.

One night, as they set up camp near a crystal-clear lake, Elara had a particularly intense dream. She saw herself standing before Lilith, a powerful aura surrounding them both. The sorceress's eyes were filled with anger and sadness, her voice a haunting echo.

"You cannot break the curse, child. You do not understand the forces at play."

Elara awoke with a start, her heart pounding. She looked over at Malachi, who was watching her with concern.

"Another dream?" he asked, his voice gentle.

She nodded, taking a deep breath. "Yes. It was Lilith. She said I can't break the curse, that I don't understand the forces at play."

Malachi's expression grew serious. "Lilith is trying to intimidate you. She knows how close we are and is desperate to stop us. We must not let her fear cloud our resolve."

Elara squeezed his hand, finding strength in his words. "You're right. We will find the Heart of Shadows and end this curse once and for all."

The next day, they reached the entrance to a hidden cave, its entrance obscured by thick vines and ancient runes. The air was heavy with magic, and Elara could feel the pulse of the Heart of Shadows within.

"This is it," Malachi said, his voice filled with determination. "Are you ready?"

Elara nodded, her resolve unwavering. "Together, we can do this."

They entered the cave, the darkness swallowing them whole. As they ventured deeper, the air grew colder, and the whispers of shadows grew louder.

The walls were lined with intricate carvings, depicting scenes of battles and powerful sorcerers.

At the heart of the cave, they found it—the Heart of Shadows. It was a large, black crystal, pulsating with dark energy. The sight of it filled Elara with a mixture of awe and dread.

This was the source of Lilith's power, the key to breaking Malachi's curse.

As they approached the crystal, a figure materialized before them—Lilith. Her presence was commanding, her eyes filled with a mix of anger and sorrow.

"You have come far, Elara," she said, her voice echoing through the cavern. "But you do not understand the true cost of what you seek to do."

Elara stood her ground, her voice steady. "I understand enough. You have caused enough pain and suffering. It ends here."

Lilith's eyes flashed with anger. "You think you can break the curse with love and determination? You are naive. The forces at play are far greater than you can comprehend."

Malachi stepped forward, his eyes blazing with determination. "We will not be intimidated by your threats, Lilith. Your time is over."

With a wave of her hand, Lilith unleashed a wave of dark energy, but Elara and Malachi were ready. Drawing upon her newfound powers, Elara created a shield of light, deflecting the attack. The two forces clashed, the cave filled with blinding light and shadow.

In the midst of the battle, Elara remembered the prophecy. "Through love and sacrifice," she whispered to herself. She realized what needed to be done.

"Malachi, we need to combine our powers," she shouted over the roar of magic. "Together, we can destroy the Heart of Shadows."

He nodded, understanding immediately. They joined hands, their combined energy creating a powerful aura. With a final burst of strength, they directed their magic at the Heart of Shadows. The crystal began to crack, the dark energy within it growing unstable.

Lilith screamed in rage, her form flickering as the source of her power was destroyed. "No! You cannot do this!"

But it was too late. With a final, resounding crack, the Heart of Shadows shattered, releasing a blinding light that filled the cave. Lilith's form dissolved into the shadows, her screams echoing into silence.

As the light faded, Elara and Malachi stood in the aftermath, their hands still clasped. The curse was broken, and the oppressive darkness lifted.

"It's over," Malachi said, his voice filled with awe and relief.

Elara nodded, tears of joy streaming down her face. "We did it. The curse is broken."

They embraced, the weight of their journey falling away. Their love had triumphed over darkness, and their future was now filled with light.

Chapter 5: The Village's Reckoning

Returning to Eldenwood was a bittersweet moment for Elara and Malachi. The village, once shrouded in suspicion and fear, now stood on the cusp of a new beginning. News of their victory over Lilith spread quickly, and the villagers gathered to witness their return.

The elder, whose mistrust had fueled much of the village's fear, stood at the forefront, his expression unreadable. Elara and Malachi approached him, their heads held high.

"We have broken the curse," Elara announced, her voice carrying the strength of their journey. "The darkness that threatened us is gone."

The elder looked at them, his gaze lingering on Malachi. "And what of the prince? Is he free from the curse?"

Malachi stepped forward, his presence no longer shadowed by dark magic. "I am free, thanks to Elara. Our love has broken the curse and defeated Lilith."

Murmurs of astonishment and relief spread through the crowd. The villagers, once fearful and suspicious, began to see Elara and Malachi in a new light. They had not only saved the village but had also proven the power of love and sacrifice.

The elder bowed his head, a gesture of respect and remorse. "I was wrong to doubt you, Elara. You have shown great courage and strength. The village owes you both a debt of gratitude."

With the elder's acknowledgement, the tension that had gripped Eldenwood began to dissipate. The villagers came forward, offering apologies and thanks, their hearts open to the possibility of a brighter future.

That night, a grand celebration took place in the village square. Lanterns were hung, music filled the air, and laughter echoed through the streets. Elara and Malachi danced together, their love a beacon of hope and renewal.

As the festivities continued, Elara found herself standing before the statue erected in their honor.

She felt a profound sense of peace, knowing that their journey had not only broken the curse but had also healed the wounds of the past.

Malachi joined her, his arm wrapping around her waist. "This is only the beginning," he said, his voice filled with promise. "Together, we can rebuild and create a future filled with light and love."

Elara nodded, her heart swelling with joy. "Yes, together."

Chapter 6: Rebuilding Trust

In the weeks that followed, Eldenwood began to heal. The villagers, inspired by Elara and Malachi's bravery, worked together to rebuild and strengthen their community. The elder, now a changed man, led with wisdom and compassion, guiding the village towards a brighter future.

Elara and Malachi dedicated themselves to helping the village. Elara used her magical abilities to restore the land, ensuring bountiful harvests and protecting the village from future threats. Malachi, with his knowledge of governance, helped to establish fair and just systems, ensuring that everyone in the village had a voice.

Their love, once seen as forbidden, became a symbol of hope and resilience. The villagers, who had once feared and mistrusted them, now looked to them as leaders and protectors. Eldenwood thrived under their guidance, becoming a place of harmony and prosperity.

One evening, as they sat together in their cottage, Elara looked at Malachi, her eyes filled with love and gratitude. "I never imagined that our journey would lead us here," she said softly.

Malachi smiled, his hand gently caressing her cheek. "Our love has brought us through the darkest of times. Now, it's time to embrace the light and build a future together."Elara nodded, feeling a deep sense of contentment. "And we will, Malachi. We will."

Chapter 7: A New Dawn

With the curse broken and Eldenwood flourishing, Elara and Malachi turned their attention to the larger world. They knew that their story was not unique—many other lands were plagued by dark forces and curses. Together, they decided to use their powers and knowledge to help others, to spread the light they had found.

Their first journey took them to the neighboring kingdom of Thalor, where a cruel sorcerer had seized power and plunged the land into darkness. Elara and Malachi, with their combined strength and unwavering love, faced the sorcerer head-on. Through their bravery and magic, they were able to overthrow the tyrant and restore peace to Thalor.

As they traveled from one land to another, their reputation grew. They became known as the "Bringers of Light," heroes who fought against darkness and injustice. Their love, a powerful and unbreakable force, inspired others to stand up against tyranny and believe in the possibility of a brighter future.

With each victory, their bond grew stronger. They faced countless challenges and dangers, but their love and determination saw them through every trial. Together, they forged alliances with other kingdoms and gathered a loyal group of followers who believed in their cause.

One of their most trusted allies was Aiden, a skilled warrior with a heart of gold. He had once been a soldier in the army of Thalor, and after witnessing Elara and Malachi's courage, he pledged his loyalty to them. His strategic mind and unwavering loyalty made him an invaluable asset in their fight against darkness.

In their travels, they also met Lena, a healer with a deep connection to nature. Her gentle spirit and powerful healing abilities provided much-needed support to their growing band of rebels. With Aiden and Lena by their side, Elara and Malachi felt more confident in their mission than ever before.

As they continued their quest, they uncovered ancient prophecies and hidden truths about the origins of the dark forces they fought against. They learned that Lilith had not been acting alone—she had been part of a larger network of dark sorcerers who sought to plunge the world into eternal night.

Determined to stop this sinister group, Elara and Malachi focused their efforts on finding the leaders of this dark network. Their journey took them to the far reaches of the known world, where they faced formidable enemies and uncovered powerful artifacts that aided them in their quest.

One such artifact was the Crystal of Light, a powerful gem that had been hidden away for centuries. Legends spoke of its ability to amplify the power of those who wielded it, making it a coveted prize for both good and evil forces. Elara and Malachi knew that if they could find the Crystal of Light, it would greatly enhance their chances of defeating the dark sorcerers.

Their search for the crystal led them to the ancient city of Elaria, a place shrouded in mystery and legend. The city was said to be protected by powerful enchantments, making it nearly impossible to find. But with the help of Aiden's tactical expertise and Lena's knowledge of ancient lore, they finally located the hidden entrance to Elaria.

As they ventured into the city, they were met with awe-inspiring sights—towering spires, intricate carvings, and a palpable sense of magic in the air. But they also faced numerous challenges, including traps and guardians that had been placed to protect the city's secrets.

After navigating through these obstacles, they finally reached the heart of Elaria, where the Crystal of Light was kept. The crystal radiated a brilliant light that filled the room, and as Elara approached it, she felt a surge of power coursing through her veins.

"With this, we can defeat them," Malachi said, his voice filled with hope.

Elara nodded, her eyes reflecting the crystal's light. "We will use this power to end the darkness once and for all."

Chapter 8: The Final Battle

Armed with the Crystal of Light, Elara, Malachi, and their allies prepared for the final confrontation with the dark sorcerers. They knew that this would be their most dangerous mission yet, but they were ready to face whatever challenges lay ahead.

Their journey led them to the Shadowlands, a desolate and treacherous region where the dark sorcerers had gathered their forces. The air was thick with malevolent energy, and the ground seemed to pulse with dark magic.

As they approached the sorcerers' stronghold, they were met with fierce resistance. The dark sorcerers had summoned creatures of shadow and darkness to defend their domain, and the battle that ensued was intense and brutal.

Elara and Malachi fought side by side, their combined powers creating a formidable force that cut through the enemy ranks. Aiden and Lena, along with the rest of their loyal followers, provided crucial support, their skills and bravery turning the tide of the battle in their favor.

But the dark sorcerers were not easily defeated. Their leader, a powerful and malevolent sorcerer named Kael, stepped forward to face Elara and Malachi. His eyes glowed with dark energy, and his presence radiated a sense of overwhelming power.

"You think you can defeat me with that pitiful crystal?" Kael sneered, his voice dripping with contempt.

Elara held the Crystal of Light aloft, its brilliance illuminating the battlefield. "We will stop you, Kael. Your reign of darkness ends here."

Kael unleashed a torrent of dark magic, but Elara and Malachi stood their ground. With the Crystal of Light amplifying their powers, they fought back with a force that matched Kael's fury. The battle raged on, the air crackling with energy as light and darkness clashed.

In the midst of the chaos, Elara felt a strange sense of clarity. She realized that the power of the Crystal of Light was not just about strength—it was about hope, love, and the unwavering belief in a better future. Drawing upon these feelings, she channeled the crystal's energy into a powerful spell.

"Together, Malachi," she said, her voice steady
and filled with determination.

Malachi nodded, understanding her intent. They
combined their magic, creating a beam of pure
light that pierced through Kael's dark defenses.
The sorcerer screamed in agony as the light
enveloped him, his form disintegrating into
nothingness.

With Kael's defeat, the remaining dark sorcerers
fled, their power broken. The Shadowlands
began to heal, the oppressive darkness lifting to
reveal a landscape filled with potential and new
life.

As the sun rose on a new day, Elara and Malachi
stood together, their hearts filled with hope and
determination. They had faced the darkness and
emerged victorious, their love and courage
lighting the way for others to follow.

Chapter 9: A World Reborn

With the defeat of Kael and the dark sorcerers,
the world began to heal. The lands that had
been plagued by darkness and fear slowly
returned to life, and the people, inspired by Elara

and Malachi's bravery, worked together to rebuild and create a future filled with hope and light.

Elara and Malachi, now hailed as heroes, continued their journey to bring peace and prosperity to the world.

They traveled to distant lands, sharing their story and helping to unite the various kingdoms in a common cause. Their love, a symbol of resilience and strength, inspired others to believe in the power of unity and hope.

In Eldenwood, the village that had once been their home, Elara and Malachi found a place of peace and reflection. They were welcomed back with open arms, the villagers now understanding the true depth of their sacrifice and courage.

The elder, who had once been their greatest critic, now stood as their staunchest supporter. "You have shown us the power of love and determination," he said, his voice filled with respect. "We are forever grateful for what you have done."

Elara and Malachi, humbled by the elder's words, knew that their journey was far from over. There were still many challenges to face, but they were ready to meet them head-on, their hearts filled with the promise of a brighter future.

Chapter 10: Legacy of Light

As the years passed, Elara and Malachi's legacy grew. They established schools of magic and knowledge, where people from all walks of life could learn and harness their abilities for the greater good. They fostered alliances between kingdoms, ensuring that the world remained united in the face of any future threats.

Their children, born into a world of light and hope, inherited their parents' strength and determination. They grew up hearing tales of their parents' bravery and the power of love and sacrifice. Inspired by these stories, they dedicated themselves to continuing their parents' work, spreading the message of hope and unity.

Elara and Malachi, though no longer at the forefront of the battles, remained deeply involved in the world they had helped to create. They served as advisors and mentors, guiding the next generation of leaders and heroes.

One evening, as they sat together on the balcony of their home in Eldenwood, Elara looked out at the sunset, her heart filled with peace. "We have come so far, Malachi," she said, her voice soft and filled with emotion.

Malachi took her hand, his eyes reflecting the colors of the setting sun. "Yes, we have. And it all began with a dream and a curse."

Elara smiled, leaning into his embrace. "Our love has created a world of light and hope. And that is a legacy that will endure forever."

Chapter 11: Eternal Love

As the years turned into decades, Elara and Malachi's bond remained as strong as ever. Their love, forged in the fires of battle and tempered by the trials they had faced, became a timeless beacon of hope and strength. They continued to inspire those around them, their story a testament to the power of love and the human spirit.

One evening, as they walked hand in hand through the village of Eldenwood, they were greeted by the smiles and waves of the villagers. The once small and fearful community had grown into a thriving and vibrant place, filled with joy and prosperity.

Elara and Malachi stopped at the statue erected in their honor, a symbol of their journey and the legacy they had created. They looked up at the stone figures, their hearts swelling with pride and gratitude.

"We have done so much, Malachi," Elara said, her voice filled with emotion. "But I feel that our journey is not yet complete."

Malachi nodded, his eyes filled with the same determination that had carried them through their many trials. "There is always more to do, more light to bring into the world. And we will face it together, as we always have."

Their children Chapter 11: Eternal Love (continued)

Their children, now grown and embarking on their own journeys, followed in their parents' footsteps.

Each had inherited a unique blend of Elara's magical abilities and Malachi's strategic mind. They traveled to new lands, helped those in need, and spread the ideals of unity and hope that their parents had instilled in them.

One evening, as Elara and Malachi strolled through the village of Eldenwood, they were joined by their eldest son, Alaric. A strong and compassionate leader, Alaric had recently returned from a mission in a distant land where he had helped to mediate peace between warring factions.

"Mother, Father," Alaric began, his voice filled with respect and admiration. "I wanted to share with you the stories I have heard in my travels. Tales of your bravery and the legacy you have left behind. People everywhere speak of you with reverence."

Elara smiled, her heart swelling with pride. "It is heartening to know that our efforts have made a lasting impact."

Malachi nodded, his eyes reflecting a sense of fulfillment. "We always knew that our journey was bigger than just us. It was about creating a world where love and hope could thrive."

Alaric looked at his parents, his eyes filled with determination. "I want to continue your work, to ensure that the light you have brought into the world never fades."

Elara and Malachi embraced their son, their hearts filled with gratitude and pride. "You have our blessing, Alaric," Malachi said. "And know that we will always be here to support you, no matter where your journey takes you."

As the years passed, Elara and Malachi watched with pride as their children and grandchildren carried on their legacy. The world they had fought so hard to protect continued to flourish, a testament to their enduring love and the sacrifices they had made

Chapter 12: The Final Journey

As they grew older, Elara and Malachi decided to take one last journey together. They wanted to visit the places that had been significant in their lives and reflect on the journey they had taken.

Their first stop was the forest where they had first met, the place where their love story had begun. The forest, once dark and foreboding, was now a place of beauty and tranquility. The trees stood tall and proud, their leaves whispering secrets of the past.

As they walked hand in hand through the forest, Elara felt a deep sense of peace. "This is where it all began," she said, her voice filled with nostalgia.

Malachi squeezed her hand, his eyes filled with love. "And it is where our love will endure forever."

Their next stop was the cave where they had found the Heart of Shadows. The cave, once a place of darkness and danger, now held a quiet serenity. The broken crystal, a symbol of their victory, still lay in the center of the cave, its pieces glimmering faintly in the light.

"We overcame so much here," Elara said, her voice tinged with awe. "

It was our greatest test."

Malachi nodded, his eyes reflecting the memory of that fateful battle. "And it was here that we truly understood the power of our love."

Their final destination was the village of Eldenwood. As they approached the village, they were greeted by the smiles and waves of the villagers. The once small and fearful community had grown into a thriving and vibrant place, filled with joy and prosperity.

Elara and Malachi stood before the statue erected in their honor, a symbol of their journey and the legacy they had created. They looked up at the stone figures, their hearts swelling with pride and gratitude.

"We have done so much, Malachi," Elara said, her voice filled with emotion. "But I feel that our journey is not yet complete."served as advisors and mentors, guiding the next generation of leaders and heroes.

Chapter 13: A New Beginning

One crisp morning, as Elara and Malachi walked through Eldenwood, they came across a group of young children playing near the village square. Among them was a little girl with bright, curious eyes who reminded them of Elara in her youth.

The girl ran up to them, her eyes wide with admiration. "Are you really the heroes who saved our village?" she asked, her voice filled with wonder.

Elara knelt down, smiling warmly at the child. "Yes, we are. But we didn't do it alone. We had many friends and allies who helped us along the way."

Malachi joined her, his eyes twinkling with affection. "And one day, you too can be a hero. All it takes is courage, kindness, and the belief that you can make a difference."

The girl's eyes sparkled with excitement. "I want to be just like you when I grow up!"

Elara and Malachi exchanged a look, their hearts filled with hope for the future. "You can be anything you want to be," Elara said gently.

"Always remember that the power to change the world lies within you."

As the girl ran back to join her friends, Elara and Malachi stood together, watching the children play. They knew that their legacy would continue, carried on by the next generation.

Epilogue: Forever in the Light

Elara and Malachi lived out their days in Eldenwood, surrounded by the love and gratitude of the people they had saved. Their home became a place of pilgrimage, where people from all over the world came to hear their story and be inspired by their journey.

They spent their twilight years in peace, reflecting on the incredible life they had shared. Their love, a beacon of light, continued to shine brightly, guiding others toward hope and unity.

One evening, as the sun set over Eldenwood, Elara and Malachi sat together on their porch, holding hands. They watched the sky turn

shades of orange and pink, a beautiful reminder of the light they had brought into the world.

"Do you remember the first time we met?" Elara asked, her voice soft and filled with fond memories.

Malachi smiled, his eyes twinkling with love. "How could I forget? It was the beginning of everything."

They sat in comfortable silence, their hearts beating in unison. As the stars began to twinkle in the night sky, they knew that their love would endure forever, a timeless legacy that would continue to inspire generations to come.

And so, Elara and Malachi's story became a legend, a tale of love, bravery, and the unbreakable bond between two souls. Their legacy lived on in the hearts of all who heard their story, a shining example of the power of love and the enduring strength of the human spirit.

In the end, Elara and Malachi found peace in knowing that they had made a lasting impact on the world. Their journey, filled with trials and triumphs, had led to a brighter, more hopeful future for all. And their love, eternal and unwavering, remained a beacon of light for generations to come.

The End